Intermediat
Oral Ski

J. C. TEM
and
KEITH NETTL

Students' Book

H·E·B

HEINEMANN EDUCATIONAL BOOKS
LONDON

Heinemann Educational Books Ltd
LONDON EDINBURGH MELBOURNE AUCKLAND TORONTO
HONG KONG SINGAPORE KUALA LUMPUR
IBADAN NAIROBI JOHANNESBURG LUSAKA
NEW DELHI KINGSTON

Intermediate Oral Skills is published together with an accompanying *Teachers' Book* (ISBN 0 435 28744 3) and recording available on *reel-to-reel tape* (ISBN 0 435 28745 1) or *cassette tape* (ISBN 0 435 28746 X).

ISBN 0 435 28743 5

First published 1977

Published by Heinemann Educational Books Ltd.
48 Charles Street, London W1X 8AH
Printed and bound in Great Britain by
Biddles Ltd., Martyr Road, Guildford, Surrey

Contents

Acknowledgements

The authors and publishers would like to thank the following for permission to reproduce illustrations:

British Railways Board (p. 51), Coloursport Ltd (p. 55), Aerofilms (p. 23), Progress Advertising Limited (p. 63), London Transport (p. 11), Chris Gilbert for photographs on pages 7, 15, 19, 27, 31, 35, 39, 43, 47, 59.

UNIT 1

What Time is it?

Section A: Listening Comprehension

1 We know that Maria was arriving in London because of
   A the parks
   B the river
   C the lights of the city
   D the name of the airport

2 As the plane landed, Maria was thinking about
   A how she was going to live in England
   B how she was going to get on with Tom and Jane
   C how she was going to get on with Mr and Mrs Clark
   D how she was going to like England

3 People in the cabin had difficulty putting their coats on because
   A they could not find them
   B there was not enough space
   C the plane was still moving
   D there was not enough time

4 Maria was annoyed because
   A everything took a long time
   B she had to walk to the terminal
   C she had to pass through Customs
   D she had to collect her baggage

5 When she found no one she knew, Maria was
   A angry
   B uncertain what to do
   C angry and uncertain what to do
   D sad and uncertain what to do

Section B: Dialogue

Arrivals Lounge, Heathrow Airport, London

AIRLINE OFFICIAL: What's the trouble, Miss? You look puzzled.

MARIA: Yes, I can't understand the time. I thought my flight arrived at 21.50, but the clock says only 21.10 now.

AIRLINE OFFICIAL: That's right, ten past nine, and I expect you waited a few minutes for your baggage.

MARIA: Yes, a long time.

AIRLINE OFFICIAL: I think I can see what has happened. Until yesterday we had British Summer Time here, but early this morning we changed to GMT – Greenwich Mean Time: we put our clocks and watches back one hour.

MARIA: Oh, I see. Perhaps that's why my friends aren't here yet. I expected to come a week ago, then I changed my plans. I forgot that the time was different.

AIRLINE OFFICIAL: This young man coming now seems to know you. Is he your friend?

MARIA: Oh yes, thank you. Tom!

TOM: Maria, it's good to see you, and you're early.

MARIA: Yes, the time I told you was British Summer Time, but I think your summer has finished.

TOM: Well, our summer finished a few weeks ago, actually. It's just Summer *Time* that finished last night. Anyway, come and meet the others – they're in the car outside.

MARIA: Thank you. It's nice to be here.

Section C: Picture

Picture Cues

The time is . . . /It is (It's)
3 a.m./3 o'clock in the morning/03.00 (usually spoken as 'o three hundred hours' or 'o three hours' in station announcements etc.)
9 a.m./9 o'clock in the morning/09.00
12 noon/midday/12.00
3 p.m./3 o'clock in the afternoon/15.00
9 p.m./9 o'clock in the evening /21.00
11 p.m./11 o'clock at night/23.00
Midnight/12 midnight/24.00

6.5 (six five) p.m./five past six (speech and informal)/18.05 (eighteen-o-five) (timetables etc.)
6.15 (six fifteen)/a quarter past six/18.15 (eighteen fifteen)
6.21 (six twenty-one)/twenty-one minutes past six/18.21
6.30 (six thirty)/half past six/18.30
6.45 (six forty-five)/a quarter to seven/18.45
6.53 (six fifty-three)/seven minutes to seven/18.53

London noon G.M.T.

Washington a.m.

Mexico a.m.

Buenos Aires Rio de Janeiro a.m.

Peking p.m.

Cairo Athens p.m.

Paris Rome Madrid p.m.

Tokyo p.m.

Section D: Situations

1 The passenger sitting next to you in an aircraft taking you to Britain asks you what you are going to do there. What do you reply?

Cues

I'm going to London (etc.) to . . . .
see friends/get a job/work as a . . . /study English
I'm going to live/stay with . . . .

2 On an aircraft in which you are flying home from Britain, the passenger sitting next to you asks you what you did while living or staying there. What do you reply?

Cues

lived/stayed/worked/studied/saw/met

3 On arriving in England, what do you say first to your friend Jo who comes to the airport or station to meet you?

Cues

how are you, Jo?
nice/good to see you/to be here
I'm glad to be here

4 Tell a friend who is going to the theatre with you what time to meet you and when the play will begin (7.30 p.m.) and end.

5 Tell a friend who is going on a train journey from London to Manchester with you what time to meet you at Euston Station, when the train will leave (09.55) and when it will arrive in Manchester (2 hours 40 minutes later).

UNIT 2

The Wrong Line

Section A: Listening Comprehension

1 Maria's feeling on entering the Underground was one of
- A great annoyance
- B terror
- C regret
- D slight fear

2 To travel to Piccadilly Circus, Maria had to pay
- A £1
- B 70p
- C 30p
- D 50p

3 Maria caught a train
- A immediately
- B after a long time
- C within an hour
- D within a few minutes

4 Maria got out at Earls Court in order to
- A change trains
- B visit an old station
- C study her Underground map
- D look at the indicators

5 When she got on the next train, Maria
- A knew it was going to Piccadilly Circus
- B hoped it was going to Piccadilly Circus
- C decided not to go to Piccadilly Circus
- D decided to go to Notting Hill Gate

Section B: Dialogue

MARIA: Excuse me, I wonder if you could help me, please.

TICKET COLLECTOR: Certainly. What's the problem?

MARIA: I want to go to Piccadilly Circus. I changed at Earls Court but I think I'm on the wrong line.

TICKET COLLECTOR: Yes, you went a bit wrong at Earls Court. You caught a District Line train, but what you need is the Piccadilly Line.

MARIA: Must I go back to Earls Court?

TICKET COLLECTOR: No. From here it's easier to take the Central Line east-bound from Platform 4. Change at Oxford Circus to the Bakerloo Line, south-bound. Piccadilly Circus is the first stop from there.

MARIA: Thank you very much. It was silly of me to get on the wrong train.

TICKET COLLECTOR: Don't worry. Visitors often find the Underground difficult at first. You'll soon get used to the Tube.

MARIA: I certainly hope so.
(*walking away, to herself*) The Central Line from Platform 4, then change at Oxford Circus to the Bakerloo . . . .

Section C: Picture

Picture Cues

the Underground/the Tube
the Piccadilly Line, the Victoria Line, etc.
Pimlico is on the Victoria Line
How can/would I get to Pimlico?
Can you tell me how . . . ?
You can/would get there by taking the (Victoria) Line.
You can/would get there by taking the (District) Line and changing to the (Victoria) Line at (Victoria).
For Pimlico, change at Victoria

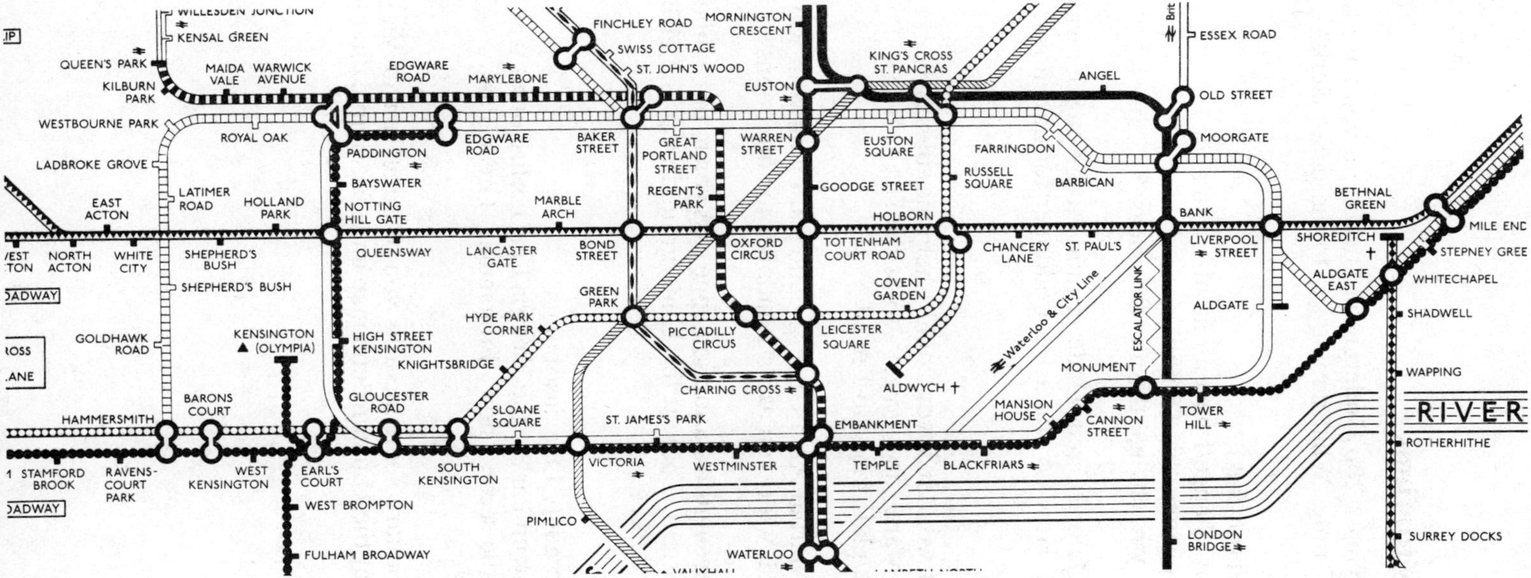

THE LONDON UNDERGROUND

Lines: VICTORIA, CENTRAL, CIRCLE, DISTRICT, METROPOLITAN, NORTHERN, BAKERLOO, PICCADILLY

FLEET

East London Section

Peak journeys only
Main service-BR

Interchange with other Underground Lines

Interchange with British Rail

▲ Exhibition Service only

† Open during Monday to Friday rush hours only

Certain Stations are closed at Weekends and during Public Holidays

Section D: Situations

1 You are buying a 20p Underground ticket but you have to change a £5 note. What do you say to the ticket clerk?

Cues

I'm sorry (about this)
I haven't any change/I haven't anything smaller
I'll have to change this £5 note
Can/could   you change this for me, please?

2 You are at Oxford Circus Underground station on your way to St Paul's. How do you ask a Londoner for directions?

Cues

Excuse me
Could you/I wonder if you could   help me, please
I'm trying/I want   to   go/get   to St Paul's
Which   line/platform   do I need

3 You are at Marble Arch Underground station on your way to Euston. How do you ask a Londoner for directions?

4 At South Kensington station someone asks you to direct him to Warren Street. Look at the Underground map and give simple directions.

Cues

Take the Piccadilly Line east-bound
Change at Green Park to the Victoria Line north-bound Warren Street's the second stop   From/after   Green Park

5 At Russell Square someone asks you to direct her to Victoria. Look at the Underground map and give simple directions.

UNIT 3

Off Colour

Section A: Listening Comprehension

1 On weekdays Maria usually got up about
  A 7.15 C 7.30
  B 8.00 D 7.45
2 On this particular morning Maria felt
  A hot C hot and unwell
  B cold D cold and unwell
3 When she realised that Maria was ill, Mrs Clark
  A did not know what to do
  B behaved in a nervous way
  C behaved in a sensible way
  D was very worried
4 Missing the film made Maria feel
  A very sad C very upset
  B slightly sad D very angry
5 Maria thought that it would be difficult
  A getting to the doctor's
  B missing college
  C understanding the doctor
  D talking to the doctor

Section B: Dialogue

DOCTOR: Good morning. You're a new patient, I think. What's the trouble?

MARIA: Sometimes I feel cold and sometimes hot. I have a headache and a stomach-ache.

DOCTOR: Yes, you look a bit off colour.

MARIA: What colour, please?

DOCTOR: Sorry – what I said was 'off colour'. It's a phrase we use to describe how someone looks or feels when he or she is unwell. Put this thermometer under your tongue, and we'll try to be more scientific! When did this start?

MARIA: I felt very tired last night when I went to bed, then I felt really bad this morning when I woke up.

DOCTOR: Yes, I see. Now let's take a look at your temperature. Ah, just as I thought – 101.

MARIA: 101! So high?

DOCTOR: Ah yes, that must sound strange to you. We often still measure people's temperature on the Fahrenheit scale, where 98.4° is a normal blood temperature. In Centigrade your temperature is 39°, which is a bit high but not exactly boiling point!

MARIA: It isn't very bad, then?

DOCTOR: No, it isn't serious. You've got a gastric form of flu – that's short for influenza. I'll write you a prescription. Take it to the chemist's and they'll make up some medicine for you. You'd better stay at home in the warm for a day or two.

MARIA: Thank you very much, doctor. I'm feeling better already. It wasn't so difficult telling you about my illness.

DOCTOR: No, language doesn't matter too much to a doctor. After all, vets manage without language at all.

MARIA: Please, what are vets?

DOCTOR: Animal doctors. Now, I must end this English lesson and see my next patient!

Section C: Picture

Picture Cues

How do you feel?/What's wrong?/What's the trouble?
I feel ill/bad/sick/hot/cold/tired etc.
I have/I've got . . . a headache/a cold/a sore throat/influenza (flu) etc.
pain (usually worse than an ache but for a shorter time)
to examine a patient
doctor's surgery/consulting room
to have a temperature (= blood temperature above normal)
to take someone's temperature
(= measure it with a thermometer)

Section D: Situations

1 You see that one of your friends looks ill, and you ask him or her sympathetically about this.

Cues

how are you feeling/how do you feel?
you don't look very/at all well
have you been to/are you going to the doctor?

2 You visit a doctor when you are in a feverish condition. He asks you how you feel. What do you reply?

Cues

I feel ill/unwell/hot and cold/feverish (etc.)
I've got a headache (etc.)

3 You visit a doctor when you have a sore throat and feel feverish. How do you describe your condition to him?

4 One of the British family you are staying with comes to see why you have not got up at breakfast time one day. Explain that you feel unwell.

5 A friend telephones when you do not arrive at his flat as arranged. You explain that you cannot go out because you are unwell.

UNIT 4

What's Cooking

Section A: Listening Comprehension

1 Yorkshire pudding is a(n)——dish.
- A new
- B old
- C sweet
- D cold

2 How many ingredients are needed?
- A four
- B three
- C five
- D it isn't certain

3 The egg is mixed
- A with butter
- B by itself
- C with flour
- D with cream

4 The ingredients must be mixed
- A well
- B not too well
- C not at all
- D half

5 When the pudding is cooked it will look
- A round
- B square
- C four-sided
- D greasy

Section B: Dialogue

Maria has been watching a cookery demonstration in a large store. Afterwards she speaks to one of the demonstrators.

MARIA: Excuse me, but did I hear you mention something called jam puffs?

DEMONSTRATOR: Yes, that's right.

MARIA: What are they, please? Are they very English?

DEMONSTRATOR: Oh yes. They're triangles of pastry with jam in between. Shall I tell you how to make them?

MARIA: Would you? Yes, please. I'll just get out my notebook and pencil.

DEMONSTRATOR: First, roll out some puff pastry very thinly.

MARIA: Very thinly. Right.

DEMONSTRATOR: Cut it into squares and put some jam on one side. Got that?

MARIA: Yes.

DEMONSTRATOR: Fold the pastry over to make a triangle.

MARIA: Fold it. I see. Let me just get that down. (pause). Yes?

DEMONSTRATOR: Seal the edges well. Brush egg white over them and sprinkle with sugar.

MARIA: Sprinkle? S-P-R-I-N-K-L-E?

DEMONSTRATOR: Correct. Then bake in a hot oven, number 6 for 10 to 15 minutes. Shall I repeat all that?

MARIA: Yes, would you mind? Thanks very much.

Section C: Picture

Picture Cues

beater/mixer — baking tin
milk bottle — jug bowl
plastic egg box — roll fold seal

Section D: Situations

1 Tell a friend how to soft boil an egg.

Cues

Put/egg/saucepan/water
When/water boil/time/egg/three minutes

2 Explain to a friend how to hard boil an egg.

3 Someone asks you how to prepare toasted cheese. What instructions do you give?

Cues

Slice/cheese/piece/toast
Put/grill/cheese/brown

4 Give a friend instructions for grilling sausages.

Cues

grill until brown one side/turn over/grill other side

5 Tom tells Maria how to make tea. He says:

Cues

Put/boiling/teapot/heat/then empty
one teaspoonful/person/one/pot
Leave/five

UNIT 5

The Waters of Bath

Section A: Listening Comprehension

1 When Maria first woke up, she thought that the day was going to be
  A strange and unpleasant C unexpected
  B unusual and interesting D satisfactory

2 Bath is famous for
  A art and history C history and architecture
  B streets and shops D art and architecture

3 In the past, people came to Bath mainly to
  A see the Baths C visit the Pump Room
  B live in fine houses D improve their health

4 Maria's feeling in Bath was one of
  A disappointment C admiration
  B sadness D expectation

5 The day seemed to Maria
  A a little too long C not quite long enough
  B much too long D much too short

Section B: Dialogue

Maria and Elizabeth are in the Roman Baths in Bath.

GUIDE: In a moment you'll be able to walk through those doors in front of you and feel the steam rising from the hot springs.

ELIZABETH: How hot is the water? What is the exact temperature?

GUIDE: It's 49 degrees Centigrade.

MARIA: Is it always the same?

GUIDE: Yes, it never changes. Every minute 1600 litres of hot water pour out of the earth. That makes over 800 million litres a year.

ELIZABETH: What will it feel like in the steam chamber?

GUIDE: Pretty hot! You could cook a meal in there. In you go.

A few minutes later, in the eighteenth-century Pump Room above the Baths:

ELIZABETH: Phew, that's better, though I'm still sweating. I couldn't see when we came out because my glasses were steamed up. What did you think of it?

MARIA: It was unusual. I've never felt so hot before.

ELIZABETH: Well, now you can have another new experience. Let's taste the famous water. Here's a glass. Hold it under the fountain.

MARIA (*drinking*) Oh, it tastes rather strange.

ELIZABETH (*drinking*) Yes, it hasn't got a very strong taste – not much taste at all, really, just warm and flat.

MARIA: Will it be good for us, d'you think?

ELIZABETH: Well, it ought to be. People have come to Bath for at least two thousand years because they thought this water would give them good health.

MARIA: That's true, but it doesn't make the water taste any better!

Section C: Picture

Picture Cues

aerial photograph   taken from the air
architecture   layout   town planning
building(s)   house(s)
terrace   street   square   circus   crescent
Georgian/eighteenth-century   style
straight   curved   round/circular

Section D: Situations

1 You visit a sauna bath for the first time with a friend. What do you say to your friend about how you feel in the steam?

Cues

Phew!/Gosh!/My goodness! etc.
I feel hot/isn't it hot?/it's boiling hot
I'm sweating/boiling
I've never felt so hot before

2 You have visited a docks and been taken into the cold storage. Describe to a friend later how you felt at a temperature of −10 degrees C.

Cues

I/it (the place, the ice, etc.) felt very cold
freezing cold/bitterly cold
I nearly froze
I've never felt . . . .

3 You are in a restaurant eating food you do not usually have (e.g. a strong curry). Tell your friend, who is eating something different, about the taste of your curry (etc.).

Cues

it tastes good/hot/unusual
hot/strong/spicy/sour/mild/sweet
I've never had/tasted anything like this before/in my life

4 You are watching a beautiful sunset from the top of a hill. What do you say to the person who is with you?

Cues

it looks beautiful (etc.)
what a beautiful (etc.) sight!
I've never seen such a . . . .

5 You are asked by an English-speaking friend to describe an historic town or city in your own country. How do you reply?

Cues

. . . is the oldest/most interesting/most historic/most beautiful, etc., in . . . .
the most famous building is . . .
it is situated on . . . (river, hill)/near/in . . .
100 BC (before Christ) 100 AD (after Christ)
Middle Ages sixteenth century (=1500–1599)

UNIT 6

Do-it-Yourself

Section A: Listening Comprehension

1 What are the three letters?
  A TIY
  B DEY
  C TEY
  D DIY

2 When are the plans made?
  A On Saturdays
  B In the evenings
  C On weekdays
  D We aren't told

3 The passage says many couples do their own home improvements because
  A it's good exercise
  B it's both enjoyable and economical
  C it saves money
  D it's economical and healthy

4 Decorators' charges have
  A increased
  B doubled
  C trebled
  D decreased

5 Who are handymen?
  A Men only
  B Women only
  C Men and women
  D We aren't told

Section B: Dialogue

Mr Clark is in a DIY shop.

MR CLARK: How much paint will I need to cover an area of 12 square metres? I want to do up my kitchen.

SALESMAN: I'll just work it out for you. Mm . . . about 4 litres.

MR CLARK: And what will that come out at for a gloss paint?

SALESMAN: Is this to do up a room?

MR CLARK: Yes.

SALESMAN: Have you allowed for the ceiling?

MR CLARK: No, I want to put a different colour on that.

SALESMAN: Well, if you really want to cut down your costs, we've got a special gloss paint at the moment going for a pound a litre.

MR CLARK: That sounds very good.

SALESMAN: Yes, it's going up to one fifty next week.

MR CLARK: In that case I'd better see the colours and pick something out right away.

SALESMAN: Here's the colour chart. I'll leave you to make up your mind.

MR CLARK: Thanks very much.

SALESMAN: It's a pleasure.

Section C: Picture

Picture Cues

put on	room	costs
do up	wall	work out
cut down	paper	tiles
'BIG DEAL' (bargain)		ladder
gloss paint (shiny)		emulsion paint (not shiny)

HOME
CARE
CENTRE
BULK BUYING MEANS BIG BARGAINS
BIG DEAL TIME AT FADS
POLYTEX
OUR PRICE £2.49
OUR PRICE £4.49
CROWN PLUS TWO GLOSS
ONLY
£1.29 £2.99
CROWN PLUS TWO EMULSION
ONLY
£2.49 £4.49
A RANGE OF YOUNGMANS LADDERS
35%
BIG CHOICE!
BIG SAVINGS!
ANAGLYPTAS
50% OFF BOOK PRICE
68p
CRISTAL CERAMIC TILES
ONLY £1.49
ONLY £1.69
DULUX EMULSION
ONLY £4.99 £2.55
DULUX GLOSS
ONLY
£1.39

Section D: Situations

1 You want to do up your room. Ask a friend to help you.

Cues

I'm going to do up my room. I wonder if you'd like to help me/give me a hand
Have you ever done up a room before?

2 You can't work out how much wallpaper you will need for a living room. Ask a friend to help you.

Cues

Could you help me to work out how much paper I'll need for the living room?
I've measured it but I still can't work it out
How *does* one work it out?

3 You cannot work out how much paint you will need to do up your kitchen. Ask a friend to help you.

4 Ask in a DIY shop if they hire ladders. You want to paint the outside of your three-storey house.

Cues

Do you hire ladders/have ladders for hire?
It's to do up the outside of my house
It's a three-storey house
I shall need a long ladder

5 Ask in a DIY shop if they sell a good, quick-drying paint. It must also be inexpensive. You want to paint your bathroom.

UNIT 7

Incident in Oxford Street

Section A: Listening Comprehension

1 Maria bought a new suitcase because
  A she did not like her old one
  B she needed two suitcases
  C her old one was too small
  D her old one was in a bad condition

2 Mrs Clark
  A suggested
  B insisted
  C demanded
  D requested
that Maria should take the suitcase back.

3 Maria told the manager of the luggage department that
  A she wanted a new suitcase
  B she did not like the suitcase
  C the suitcase she had bought was unsatisfactory
  D she wanted her money back

4 The manager was
  A surprised
  B amused
  C thoughtful
  D helpful

5 The store detective who stopped Maria wanted to
  A help her
  B question her
  C meet her
  D greet her

Section B: Dialogue

STORE DETECTIVE: Excuse me, madam. I see that you have a new suitcase. Did you buy it in the store?

MARIA: Yes, I did.

STORE DETECTIVE: Could you show me the receipt, then, please?

MARIA: Oh dear, no I don't think they gave me a receipt today. You see, I brought one back and they gave me this one instead.

STORE DETECTIVE: Why did you bring one back?

MARIA: Well, I came here and bought one yesterday. Then I went home and found that it didn't work properly. I had to bring it back and they changed it for this one.

STORE DETECTIVE: Oh, I see. If you don't mind perhaps we could take the suitcase back to the luggage department and ask them about this.

MARIA: All right. But I'm getting tired of bringing and taking these suitcases from one place to another, and buying and changing them.

STORE DETECTIVE: I'm sorry, madam, but it's my job to make sure that people don't take anything from this store unless they have paid for it.

(In the luggage department)

STORE DETECTIVE: This young lady says that you just gave her this suitcase in exchange for one she brought back. Is this right?

MANAGER: Yes, it's quite right. I'm sorry that you were stopped, madam. This time we'll give you a new receipt: then nobody will be able to accuse you of shoplifting.

MARIA: 'Shoplifting'? What's that?

STORE DETECTIVE: It's what I have to stop people doing! A shoplifter is a person who takes something from a shop or store without paying.

MARIA: Oh, I see. Well, at least I've learned a new word!

Section C: Picture

Picture Cues

shop store (= big shop with many departments)
store detective
shopping
suitcase lock
buy/bought/bought bring/brought/brought
take/took/taken

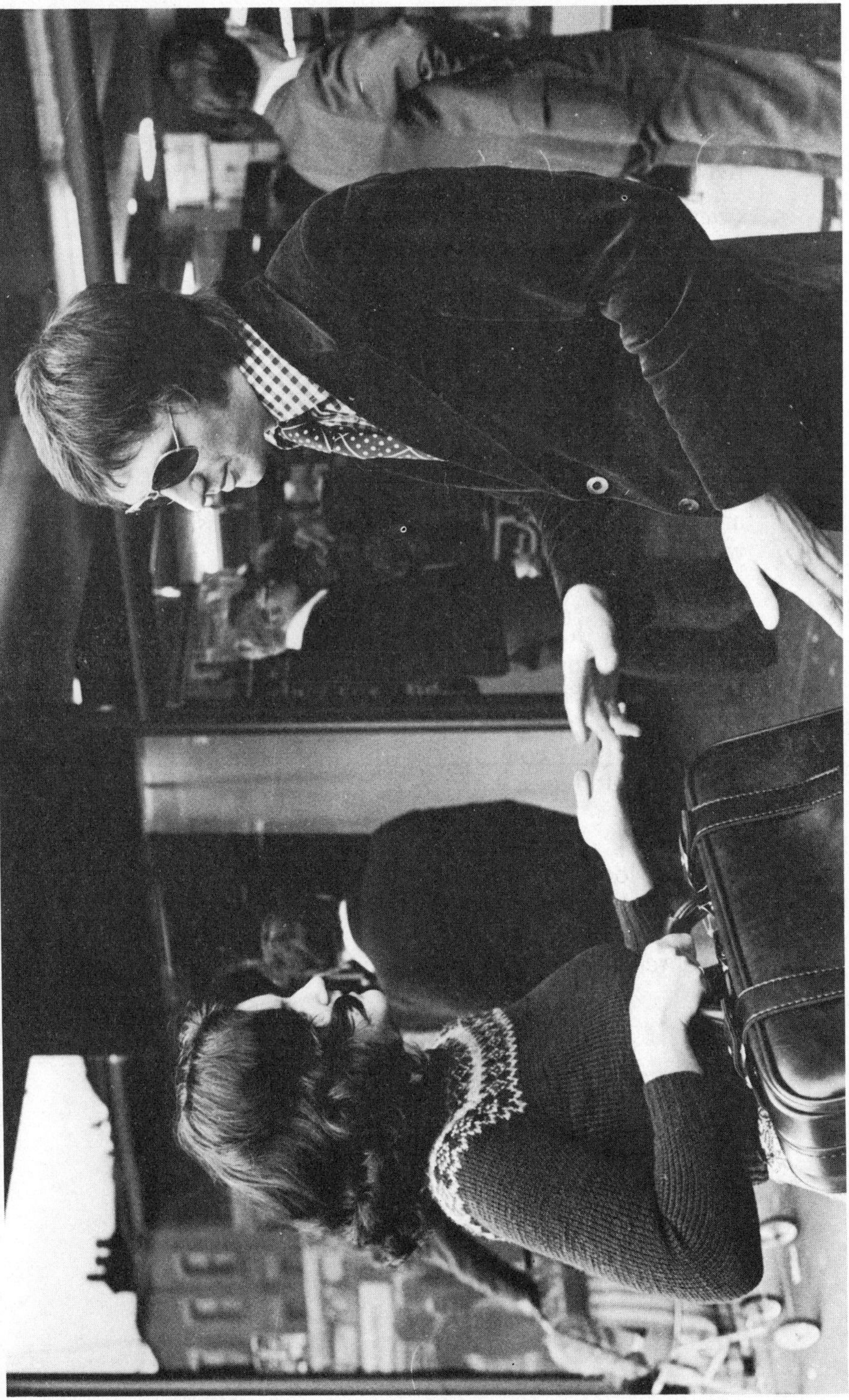

Section D: Situations

1 As you leave a store after buying a handbag, a store detective stops you and asks about it. Explain what has happened.

Cues

I've just bought . . .
I've paid for it
I bought it on the ground floor (etc.)
it cost £10/I paid £10 for it

2 As you leave a store after buying an umbrella a store detective stops you and asks about it. Explain what has happened.

3 You have bought a book which you find has some pages missing. What do you say to the bookshop assistant when you take it back?

Cues

I've brought this book back because . . .
I'd like to change it for a perfect copy
please let me have a perfect copy

4 You take a new coat back to the shop where you bought it because it has a hole in it. What do you say to the assistant?

5 You are looking after a young child, Richard. One day you take him to the shops, buy him an ice cream, and then bring him back later. Later you telephone a friend and describe exactly what you did.

UNIT 8

It's on Tape

Section A: Listening Comprehension

Maria sends a cassette to her friend Mercedes, who is also learning English.

1 Who had first suggested sending tapes in English?
- A Mercedes
- B Maria's teacher
- C Maria
- D We can't tell

2 Maria understood what people said
- A from the beginning
- B gradually
- C if they spoke clearly
- D if they spoke slowly

3 Maria is pleased because she
- A stopped studying
- B studied harder
- C continued studying
- D enjoys studying English

4 What season is it?
- A Spring
- B Summer
- C Autumn
- D Maria doesn't say

5 After six months Maria
- A may go home
- B will go home
- C won't go home
- D will speak perfectly

Section B: Dialogue

Maria goes to buy a cassette recorder. The shop assistant, S., shows her two machines – a Toyo and a Smith.

M: Which is better, do you think – the Toyo or the Smith?

S: Well the Toyo's a little bit cheaper. But the Smith's a bit bigger.

M: Which one sounds better?

S: The Toyo's got a sharper tone than the Smith.

M: I think I prefer one with a smoother tone.

S: The Smith's louder, of course, if you want a loud machine.

M: Yes, I might want something louder for certain kinds of music.

S: The Smith's certainly got a bigger speaker.

M: Which is easier to carry?

S: The Smith's a bit heavier than the Toyo. Then again the Toyo's handier in some ways. You can take the lid off.

M: Oh dear, one's bigger, the other's cheaper, one's louder, the other's more something else – I'm getting more and more confused.

S: Which one do you prefer the look of?

M: Well, the Toyo's got a nicer shape, but I like the colour of the Smith better. (*after a pause*) No, it's hopeless. I'll just have to leave it for the moment, if you don't mind.

S: Not at all, miss. It's better to be sure than sorry. Wait till you're more certain.

Section C: Picture

Picture Cues

hi-fi	tuner
record-player	pick-up
stereo	pick-up arm
(loud)speaker(s)	wave bands
treble/bass	transistor
amplifier	reel-to-reel

MARINE
RADIO
NOW ONLY £14.95
£49.95
SAVE £2
BUSH
BA 5005
£13.95
VOYAGER 3
£24
SAVE £5
HARRIER
CHIEFTAIN
RADIO
NOW ONLY £19.95
GIFT IDEAS
GIFT IDEA
PRINZSOUND
£55.95
Dixons
SONY
TA-1630
AMPLIFIER
£99.95
CHRISTMAS VALUE
SONY TC377
£189.95
£118
£104
STD 500
£49.95
SAVE £10
£29.95
PRINZSOUND
PL15
RECORD DECK
NOW ONLY £39.95

Section D: Situations

1 What do you tell a friend who asks which you think is the better way to learn English – to study with tapes in his own country or come to England?

Cues

better to
It's quicker/more practical
You're closer

2 Explain on a cassette to a friend why you would rather learn English by living with a family than living on your own.

Cues

It's –er/more ––– and it's

3 'Did you find it hard to understand what English people were saying at first?' a friend asks,

Cues

Well, it was . . . than I
They spoke . . . than I
It took me . . . than
I had to listen . . . than at school

4 Someone asks whether you prefer summer or autumn in London. Answer with your reasons.

Cues

It's (sun/bright/dry/mild/cool)
The weather's
The parks are
easier/more difficult shop/travel concert/theatre

5 Where would you prefer to live in England? In London or in the country? On a cassette to a friend briefly give the reasons for your choice.

UNIT 9

When Did You Go to the Zoo?

Section A: Listening Comprehension

1 Maria had been to the London Zoo
  A once
  B twice
  C by Tube
  D never

2 When Maria saw the advertisement she was
  A annoyed
  B surprised
  C amused
  D puzzled

3 Maria enjoyed the Zoo
  A as much as museums
  B less than museums
  C more than museums
  D but not museums

4 When did Tom see the Zoo advertisement?
  A The previous day
  B That morning
  C Several days before
  D We don't know

5 How many times has Tom been to the Zoo?
  A Twenty
  B Less than twenty
  C Forty
  D More than twenty

Section B: Dialogue

The phone rings at 5 o'clock. B *answers.*

B: 332 4709.

A: Where were you? I've been trying to get you all day.

B: I was out.

A: Yes, I know that. That's why I didn't get an answer. Where were you?

B: I was at the Zoo. I've only just got back.

A: At the Zoo! No wonder I haven't been able to get you. Did you enjoy it?

B: Yes, very much. It was fascinating. Have you ever been there?

A: I haven't been since I was a child. I enjoyed it too – except for the lions.

B: Oh didn't you like them?

A: They frightened me. But I had a ride on an elephant, and I soon forgot about them.

B: You're braver than me. I've always been afraid of elephants.

A: Were you afraid yesterday?

B: Yes, I was rather. Anyway, what have you been ringing me about all day?

Section C: Picture

Picture Cues

No, I . . . never actually . . .
Yes, I . . . often . . .
. . . Zoo/book/film
feed
They . . . Indian/Indian jungle
They . . . cages/ship/plane

Section D: Situations

1 You went to the Zoo this morning, had lunch there, and then went home. A message says a friend phoned at 10 and 11 am. Ring and tell him briefly what you were doing.

Cues

I went to/was at the Zoo this morning
I've only just got back
I had lunch there too
I had a wonderful time

2 A friend asks if you've been to any of the London museums. Choose a suitable reply, using the cues.

Cues

Yes, I've been to the Science/Natural History/Victoria and Albert Museum
I went last Monday/week/month
No, I've never been to any of the London museums
But last week I went to the Zoo

3 A friend asks if you've visited any of the London art galleries (The Tate, the National, the National Portrait). What do you answer?

4 A friend asks why you wanted to visit Hampton Court Palace, and what arrangements you made to go there. Explain.

Cues

I've always wanted to visit it
I've always been interested in Henry the Eighth
I went to a travel agent
I booked a rail trip

5 A friend asks how you learned that a new restaurant was opening. Answer using words like 'train; newspaper; advertisement' or 'two people talking'.

UNIT 10

At the Supermarket

Section A: Listening Comprehension

1 An example of 'household things and food' would be
   A Butter, cheese and eggs
   B Plates, matches, floor polish
   C Soap, rice, milk
   D Flour, sausages, beer

2 A trolley is
   A carried
   B driven
   C pushed
   D pedalled

3 The shop doesn't need a licence to sell
   A beer
   B gin
   C coke
   D rum

4 The check-out girl's arithmetic
   A needn't be good
   B must be good
   C is often bad
   D needs improving

5 The passage suggests that the last part of the shopping is
   A easy
   B slow
   C confusing
   D expensive

Section B: Dialogue

Maria sees an elderly woman trying to pick up some tins she has knocked down from a crowded shelf.

MARIA: Here, let me help you.

WOMAN: Oh, thank you so much. I do dislike shopping in these places. They seem to be full of things you didn't find in grocers' shops in the old days – wine, for example, and all these frozen goods, and Continental foods.

MARIA: Well, I'm from abroad, and this supermarket certainly has the same kinds of food and drink as I'm used to in my country.

WOMAN: Yes, it's all a bit strange to me. But it's too expensive for me to go to the little shops.

MARIA: Yes, they can't afford to charge low prices like the big shops.

WOMAN: Oh well, it's no use complaining, I suppose. It's nice to get things cheap. Thank you for helping me.

MARIA: Not at all.

Maria is at a check-out point. She says to the Cashier:

MARIA: I think you've overcharged me. You've made me pay 5p too much for soap.

CASHIER: Let me see. Oh dear. Yes, it ought to be 9p. It's usually 14p but there's a special offer. They decided to reduce it by 5p. I'll put that right.

MARIA: Thanks. Do you mind changing ten pounds?

CASHIER: Not if you don't mind having 50p pieces in your change instead of notes.

MARIA: Not a bit. It doesn't take long to spend it these days.

CASHIER: No, you're right.

Section C: Picture

Picture Cues

For –ing
to —
tin/can packet carton
basket trolley
frozen goods

Gravy and Lean Roast Beef
EXPRESS LONG LIFE MILK
from LANCA
Super Oran

Section D: Situations

1 You are ill and ring up a friend because you want some things from the shops. What do you say?

Cues

Would you mind . . .
I'm not very well
I'm sorry to bother you/be a nuisance
Could you get me some . . .

2 On hearing that a friend is unable to go out, you ring up and offer to shop for him. What do you say?

3 Some tins of soup you want in a supermarket are in a carton not yet unpacked beside the shelf. Ask an assistant to help you.

Cues

Could you . . .
Would you mind . . .

4 A friend hears you are going to the shops and asks very apologetically to get him a few things. Assure him you would be very pleased.

Cues

I'm very fond of shopping
I'd like to shop for you
I wouldn't mind at all/in the least

5 In a supermarket a woman, trying to shop, asks you very apologetically to mind her small child for a few moments. Assure her you would be very pleased.

UNIT 11

Party Talk

Section A: Listening Comprehension

1 Who was giving the party?
   A Susie
   B Sheila
   C Ann
   D Martha

2 How many guests did Tom and Maria first see?
   A Four
   B Five
   C Six
   D Seven

3 Where did Maria leave her coat?
   A In a bedroom
   B In a living room
   C In the hall
   D We aren't told

4 At first two of the guests were
   A standing apart
   B rather quiet
   C indifferent
   D unfriendly

5 Susie's friend was
   A a young man
   B a girl
   C not English
   D We aren't told

Section B: Dialogue

At the party Bill speaks to Maria.

BILL: Hello, I'm Bill. I'd heard from Ann that you were coming to the party.

MARIA: Hello. I hadn't met any of the guests before this evening – except Ann.

BILL: You're from South America, Ann said.

MARIA: Yes, that's right.

BILL: How long have you been living in London?

MARIA: About six months now.

BILL: And how long had you been learning English before you came here?

MARIA: About three years in school.

BILL: Your English is very good.

MARIA: Thank you very much.

BILL: Is London very different from what you'd thought?

MARIA: I hadn't realised it was so big. And I'd thought I'd find it easier to understand people at first than I did.

BILL: Had you ever met any English people before?

MARIA: Only one. I'd had a teacher who was English. And as I'd been able to understand him I thought I'd be able to understand everyone.

BILL: I wish I'd had a language teacher at school who'd taught me as well as yours taught you.

MARIA: Oh well, thank you again.

Section C: Picture

Picture Cues

have a drink
chat
get together
share a joke

Section D: Situations

1 Someone you meet at a party says he has read a lot about South America and he's always wanted to go there. The next day you tell a friend about the conversation.

Cues

I met a man/girl at a party last night and he/she said
A girl/man I met at a party last night said

2 Everyone in your house has gone out. You hear some strange music and knocking downstairs. By the time you get down there it has stopped. Tell some other guests at a party about the experience.

Cues

Everyone in the house
I heard
By the time I got downstairs

3 You have heard there is a sale of coats at Selfridges. By the time you get there they have all been sold. How do you tell a friend about it?

4 You would really like to give some useful addresses to someone you meet at a party, but have left your address book at home. You are sorry about this.

Cues

Isn't it silly! I've left it at home
I wish I'd brought it with me
I realised I'd left it behind the moment I got here
I'd been using it before I came out

5 You are leaving a party and the weather has become suddenly cold. Your light raincoat isn't really warm enough. What do you say?

Cues

I wish . . . something warmer
I wish . . . the weather forecast
I wish . . . my friend's car

UNIT 12

We Love Our Railways

Section A: Listening Comprehension

1 Boys used to want to be
   A astronauts
   B designers
   C engine drivers
   D computer operators

2 Today most boys play with
   A toy trains
   B small cars
   C sets
   D trains

3 The train information Maria usually received was
   A a lot
   B very little
   C very brief
   D boring

4 In the hall Mr Clark kept a(n)
   A old timetable
   B large railway map
   C book of train times
   D book about engines

5 What did Mr Clark like doing on trains?
   A eating
   B sleeping
   C looking out
   D thinking

Section B: Dialogue

MARIA: If I wanted to go to Exeter, what would be the best way to go?

MRS CLARK: Exeter. Well, let's look at the rail guide. I believe there are two ways. Yes, here we are.

MARIA: Can you understand it? If I could read that I'd think I was very clever.

MRS CLARK: Oh it's not so difficult. Now let's see. You can go from Waterloo or Paddington. It's slower from Waterloo, but if you go that way you can see the spire of Salisbury Cathedral from the train. If you leave Waterloo at eight o'clock, you'll be in Exeter at 11.57 – if the train's on time.

MARIA: And what if I went the other way – from Paddington?

MRS CLARK: If you left Paddington at 7.30, you'd be at Exeter at 10.30.

MARIA: It'll be much quicker if I go that way. I could visit Salisbury another time. But it'll be awful if I don't wake up in time – and miss the train.

MRS CLARK: If you're not too late it won't matter. You'll still be able to catch the 8.30 and arrive at 11.13.

MARIA: That's even faster, isn't it? It's less than two and three quarter hours. If I go that's the train I'll catch.

Section C: Picture

Picture Cues

She can get I'd prefer
restraurant car/dining car/buffet car
fast train/express slow/stopping train via
non-stop from Reading to Taunton
through train (no change needed)

London to Salisbury and Exeter

Miles			MX				H			A	A	J			L
							☕				✕	✕ ☕	☕		✕ ☕
0	**London Waterloo**	158 d		01 40			06 30	*06 46*	*07 46*	08 00	09 00	09 00		*09 46*	11 00
12	Surbiton	158 d					06 47		*07 39*	*07 58*	*08 58*	*08 58*		*09 39*	*10 58*
24¼	Woking ‡	158 d					07 01	*07 12*	*08 12*	08 29	09 29	09 29		*10 12*	11 29
—	**123** Reading	d					*06 56*		07 59	*07 59*	*08 59*	*08 59*		09 59	*11 20*
47¾	**Basingstoke**	158 d	00 04				07 26	07 39	08 39	08 53	09 53	09 53		10 39	11 53
55½	Overton	d						07 51	08 49					10 49	
59¼	Whitchurch (Hants)	d						07 58	08 55					10 55	
66½	Andover	d	00 24	02 58			07 47	08e11	09 04	09 15	10 15	10 15		11 04	12 15
72¾	Grateley	d						08 20	09 13					11 13	
83¾	**Salisbury**	a	00 45	03 25			08 09	08 35	09 28	09 37	10 37	10 37		11 28	12 37
—	**171** Brighton	d								*06 30*	*07 45*	*07f05*	09 00		*09 45*
—	**165** Portsmouth & Southsea	d					*05 54*			*08 00*	*08 52*	*08f56*	*09 30*		*11 00*
—	**165** Southampton	d					*06 53*			*08 53*	*09 50*	*09 50*	10 38		*11 53*
—	**Salisbury**	d		03 33		06 26	08 12			09 45	10 40	10 40	11 15		12 40
96¼	Tisbury	d				06 44	08 30								
105½	Gillingham (Dorset)	d		04c05		06 56	08 42					11 06	11 46		13 06
118¼	Sherborne	d		04c29		07 14	08 59			10 21	11 18	11 24	12 05		13 24
122¾	Yeovil Junction	d		04a40		07 22	09 07			10 30	11 26	11 32	12 13		13 34
131¾	Crewkerne	d				07 37	09 22			10 45		11 47			13 49
144¾	Axminster	d				07 53	09 38			11 10	11 57	12 03	12 39		14 05
155	Honiton	d			07 25	08 12	09 56			11 27	12 15	12 21	12 55		14 23
159½	Feniton	d			07 31	08 20	10 03								
163½	Whimple	d			07 37	08 26	10 09								
171¾	**Exeter Central**	a			07 48	08 38	10 22			11 48	12 36	12 40	13 17		14 42
172½	**Exeter St. David's**	a			07 53	08 42	10 27			11 57	12 40	12h49	13 24		14 46

London and Bristol to Torbay and Plymouth

Miles	Miles				E	G FX			K	A		Y				D	A	B	H
				☕						✕ ☕		✕ ☕		☕		☕	✕ ☕	☕	✕ ☕
0	—	**London Paddington**	117 d							07 30		08 30				08 57	09 35		
18½	—	Slough	117 d																
—	—	**117** Oxford	d							*07t14*		*07 52*				*07 52*	*09 10*		
—	—	**125** Heathrow Airport 🚌	d							*06 55*		*07 40*				*07 40*	*08 40*		
36	—	**Reading**	117, 122 d							08 02		09 01				09 27	10 06		
53	—	Newbury	122 d							08 26						09 51			
75¼	—	Pewsey	122 d																
95½	—	Westbury	122, 132 d							09 11						10 54			
115¼	—	Castle Cary	132 d													10 56			
—	—	**51** Birmingham New Street	d						*07 00*					08 20				09 15	10 15
—	—	**131** Cardiff Central	d	*06v25*				*07 10*	07 58					*09z00*				*10 10*	*10 10*
—	—	**131** Newport	d	*06v38*				*07 24*	08 11					*09z14*				*10 24*	*10 24*
—	0	**Bristol Temple Meads**	134 d	08 05				08 25	09 00					10 10				11 13	11 53
—	19	Weston-super-Mare	134 d	08 31				08 56										11 34	
—	26¾	Highbridge	d					09 07											
—	33	Bridgwater	d					09 16						10 39				11 50	
143	44¾	Taunton	d	08 59				09a32	09 40	09 55		10 38		10 56		11 20		12 07	
159	60¾	Tiverton Junction	d																
173¾	75½	**Exeter St. David's**	d	09 33			09 55		10 14	10 30		11 13		11 30		11 54	12 10	12 43	13 05
185	86¾	**138** Exmouth	a						*10 53*			*11 55*		*13 10*		*13 10*	*13 10*		
212½	114¼	**137** Barnstaple	a									*12 32*		*12 32*					
174¾	76½	Exeter St. Thomas	d				09 58												
182¼	84	Starcross	d				10 07												
184¼	86	Dawlish Warren	d				10 12												
185¾	87½	Dawlish	d	09 48			10 17		10 30					11 47		12 10		12 59	
188¾	90½	Teignmouth	d	09 54			10 23		10 36					11 53		12 16		13 04	
193¾	95½	Newton Abbot	d	10 00	10 00	10 30	10a33		10 43	10 53	11 04	11 36		12 01	12 00	12 23		13f18	
199	100¾	Torre	d																
199¾	101½	Torquay	d		10 13						11 14				12 10	12 37		13 31	
202	103¾	Paignton	a		10 20						11 20				12 16	12 45		13 39	
202½	104¼	Totnes	d			10 46				11 10				12 18					
225¾	127½	**Plymouth**	a	10 45		11 20			11 28	11 44		12 20		12 51			13 15		14 11
—	—		136 d	10 46						11 56							13 23		14 23

Section D: Situations

1 You are enquiring about a journey which can be done from either King's Cross or Liverpool Street stations in London (e.g. Cambridge). What do you say?

2 You live at Exeter and ask at St. David's Station if you will have much time to spend in London on a cheap-day return.

Cues

If I buy a cheap-day return how long . . .
What time last train back London
If I London cheap-day return

3 You want a friend to show you round an art gallery he/she knows well, and you offer to pay the fares there.

Cue

If I paid . . .

4 You may get home to London by train too late to let in a friend but you have left the key under the mat. Explain this to him. Begin: If . . .

5 Winning some money would mean you could visit several places in Britain. Say which three places you would visit first. Begin: If . . .

UNIT 13

What Kind of Football?

Section A: Listening Comprehension

1 The Clarks thought that on Saturdays Maria should avoid
 A the traffic
 B football matches in London
 C football matches in other cities
 D football fans on trains

2 Maria thought that interest in football was
 A greater in England than in her own country
 B less in England than in her own country
 C about the same in both countries
 D low in both countries

3 Mrs Clark and Elizabeth watched 'Match of the Day'
 A not very often
 B whenever they were at home
 C only when Mr Clark and Tom were in
 D only when Mr Clark and Tom were out

4 Tom and Elizabeth said that they
 A played the same game in winter
 B played the same game in summer
 C watched the same game in winter
 D watched the same game in summer

5 Maria
 A disliked soccer
 B disliked rugby
 C did not understand rugby
 D did not understand soccer or rugby

Section B: Dialogue

Maria and Tom are at Twickenham Stadium before the start of the England v. Wales rugby international.

MARIA: What's that picture the man's carrying?

TOM: It's a Welsh supporters' banner with a dragon on it. The dragon is an ancient symbol of Wales.

MARIA: The man isn't walking very steadily.

TOM: No. He's probably been drinking beer ever since he left South Wales hours ago. An enormous amount of beer is drunk at these matches.

MARIA: And what is that song?

TOM: The Welsh are all singing 'Land of My Fathers' – it's a great national song.

MARIA: They sing well.

TOM: Yes. The Welsh love music, especially this sort of singing. Every town and village in the mining valleys of South Wales has its male voice choir – and its rugby team.

MARIA: Have all these thousands of Welshmen travelled from Wales today?

TOM: No, a lot of them live in London. Think of all the people called Jones, or Davies, or Powell, or Hughes who live in London.

MARIA: I suppose so. Then there are the people living here with Scottish names like Mackintosh or MacGibbon.

TOM: Yes, it's a reminder that the English are only one of the nations of Britain. But let's get back to rugby. Here are the teams. Can you remember what I told you about tries, line-ups, and scrums?

MARIA: Not very well, but you can give me a commentary.

TOM: Not likely. I'll be cheering England. I'll give you a commentary tonight when we see the film on television.

Section C: Picture

Picture Cues

crowd	banner	score (verb and noun)
supporters	cheer	
flag	team	

Section D: Situations

1 An English person offers to take you to a soccer or rugby match. Say which you would prefer, and why.

Cues

I'd like/I'd prefer to go to . . .
I like watching . . .
I don't know much/anything about rugby
It would be interesting for me

2 An English friend asks you whether you would prefer to play tennis or to go swimming. You reply, giving a reason.

Cues

I like/I'm keen on swimming/(playing) tennis
I'm no good at swimming/(playing) tennis
I play/swim a lot/a great deal

3 Your host offers to take you to a ballet or to a Western film. Say which you would prefer, and why.

4 A friend suggests that you travel to Bristol by train one Saturday in the football season. You explain why you think this might be unwise.

5 After attending the England v. Wales international at Twickenham you telephone a friend to tell him about what the Welsh supporters did before the match.

UNIT 14

City Radio

Section A: Listening Comprehension

1 The next news on City Radio will be at
   A 7.30   C 9.00
   B 8.30   D Some other time

2 The greatest number of passengers in the airliner which crashed
   A swam to an island
   B probably died
   C escaped on life rafts
   D were rescued by helicopters

3 The Prime Minister is going to
   A The USA   C The UN
   B The USSR   D The UK

4 Good Time Holidays offer
   A a few holidays
   B some holidays of one kind
   C holidays of many different kinds
   D many cheap holidays

5 The advertisement says that girls who try HAIR BEAUTY shampoo
   A like it better than other kinds
   B like it as much as other kinds
   C think it is quite good
   D don't want to use any shampoo

Section B: Dialogue

STEWART: This is City Radio and I'm Geoff Stewart. It's time for Two-Way Talk, the phone-in show that gives you the chance to pick up your phone and talk to everyone. The number to ring is 26264. First caller, please.

CALLER: Hello Geoff. I'm June. I'm a housewife. I want to talk about prices. Most things cost too much these days. Nearly everything seems to cost much more than it did a few years ago.

STEWART: It would be good to have some examples. Can you think of any?

CALLER: Well, there's food, to begin with. We eat less, but it costs more. Then there's travel by bus and train – higher fares for shorter journeys. As for holidays, we used to have two or three a year but now we can't afford any.

STEWART: I'm sorry to hear that. I wonder whether our next caller feels the same, or whether he'll have something different to tell us. Come in, caller.

2ND CALLER: Good morning, Mr Stewart. I'm an old-age pensioner. I haven't got much money in the bank but I manage quite well.

STEWART: Have you got any advice for listeners?

2ND CALLER: Yes. Try to save a little money each week. You'll soon find that even if you haven't got a lot you've got some money when you really need it.

STEWART: That sounds very sensible. May I ask how old you are?

2ND CALLER: I'm 79. I'll be 80 in July.

STEWART: Will you really? You sound a lot younger than that. Thanks for talking to us.

Section C: Picture

Picture Cues

advertisement (advert or ad for short)
10p/40% off (=reduction of 10p or 40 per cent)
reasonable (=not too high, of prices)
latest (=newest, most modern)
special offer (=reduced price of a particular item for a short period)

MARKET PLACE

YOU GET

BETTER VALUE

AND

MORE CHOICE

at *Fine Food Supermarket*

10p. off Soap Powder this week

MANY SPECIAL OFFERS

• Branches everywhere •

MILK

is good for you

and it's not expensive

Drink some yourself

and give <u>more</u> to your children

40% OFF NORMAL PRICES!

Watches

from £8

Calculators

from £10

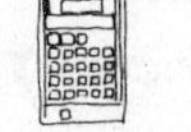

Typewriters

from £20

FANTASTIC OFFERS!

Cash or Credit Cards

WAREHOUSE SUPPLIES
480 HIGH ST. SE 31
TUBE: NEW CROSS

Clothes

by Mail Order

▷ LATEST FASHIONS

▷ NO FUSS OR QUEUES

▷ REASONABLE PRICES

▷ SHOP IN COMFORT

Send for catalogue to

HOME FASHIONS, P.O. BOX 99
NEWTOWN PR7 0BY

BUY NOW & SAVE
THESE PRICES
CANNOT LAST!

REAL LEATHER SHOES

FOR ONLY **£6~50**

This beautiful shoe has the quality of shoes costing twice or three times as much. Buy a pair or two while you have the chance.

Cash with order to: SMITH FOOTWEAR, 65 MARKET ST., BRIMSTONE B16 5NF

Section D: Situations

1 Briefly describe (as if in a radio news programme) a recent piece of world or local news.

2 You are working in an advertising agency, and have to think of a radio advert ('commercial') for a new toothpaste. Give some suggestions.

Cues

. . . is good for your teeth/does your teeth good
makes your teeth look/feel good
tastes nice(r)/good (better)/pleasant(er)

3 As Situation 2, but you are advertising holidays for Britons or Americans in your own country.

Cues

Come to beautiful/sunny/peaceful . . .
there's more/so much to do in . . .
beaches/mountains/rivers/historic cities etc.
swimming/ski-ing/sunbathing/water sports/climbing/walking/touring/sightseeing etc.
reasonable cost/it costs less than you think

4 You telephone the firm Warehouse Supplies (see Picture) and ask for more details of their watches.

Cues

what sort of watches?
what are they made of?
is there a guarantee?
how much do they cost?/what is the exact price?

5 You are taking part in a phone-in radio programme. The discussion is about road accidents. You give your view briefly.

Cues

too many cars on the road
some bad drivers/some people drive badly
fast/dangerous driving
people should drive more carefully
bad weather conditions/fog, ice, etc.

UNIT 15

High Fashion – or – Just Jeans?

Section A: Listening Comprehension

1 When Mrs Clark suggested buying clothes, Maria had
- A already made plans to do so
- B no plans about it
- C bought all she wanted
- D almost decided what to buy

2 Maria says the fashions change
- A once a year
- B every four months
- C four times a year
- D many times a year

3 Maria liked jean material because it was
- A popular and inexpensive
- B popular and hard-wearing
- C hard-wearing and inexpensive
- D expensive but popular

4 Maria was going to buy long dresses because
- A she liked the look of them
- B they would keep her warm
- C they were comfortable
- D she didn't like long skirts

5 Tom thought he would see Maria again
- A some time
- B in five years
- C once or twice
- D never

Section B: Dialogue

MRS CLARK: I've had an invitation to a fashion show. Would you like to come, Maria? It's for two.

MARIA: It's very kind of you to ask me but I'm going to Oxford Street to buy some clothes before I go back.

MRS C: No, I don't think you younger people bother about the latest fashions these days.

TOM: Well they're not really meant for us, are they. Most young people wear jeans and cheesecloth shirts, and things like that. And they don't cost half as much as some of the so-called latest fashions.

MRS C: Yes, I must say they're very practical and hard-wearing. And the shirts are very colourful. But I do like a change.

MARIA: There are the long skirts. You like those, don't you?

MRS C: Yes, there's something very attractive about them. But I wish *you'd* wear something different occasionally, Tom.

TOM: Well, I'm not a city gent, am I? I can hardly go round in a bowler hat. Anyway, I wear a suit now and again.

MRS C: Not when you're going anywhere with me.

TOM (Surprised): Oh, don't I? Well, I'll tell you what: next time we're going anywhere, I'll definitely wear a suit. How's that?

MRS C: Splendid, I'll hold you to it.

MARIA: And you can write and tell me all about it, Tom.

Section C: Picture

Picture Cues

jeans/clothing made from jean material
jacket/waistcoat
trousers
hip pockets
style cut
tight
ad/advert/advertisement joke/pun/play on words

true blue
FALMER
jeanius

Section D: Situations

1 Tell a friend what clothes you want to buy in Britain, and where you will go for them.

Cues

I want (to get) . . ./I'm looking for . . .
I'll go to/try Oxford/Carnaby Street/the big department stores

2 A friend compliments you on something you are wearing, and asks you where you got it. Make a suitable reply.

3 Describe to an assistant a coat you have seen in the window and ask for one in your size and in a different colour.

Cues

It's (a) long/short (one)
I want/Have you got a (size), only in (colour)(?)

4 Someone doing a questionnaire on clothes-buying habits stops you in the street and asks which you prefer – the latest fashion or jeans, and why. What do you reply.

5 It is 3 p.m. and you go to a dry-cleaner's to ask about their express service for a suit you want to wear that evening. What do you say.

Cues

Could you dry-clean a suit for me in time for this evening?
I want to wear this suit this evening. Could you dry-clean it before six?
If I left this suit now, would you be able/it be possible to . . .